MW01177897

This book belongs to:

_____

Published by Ladybird Books Ltd
27 Wrights Lane London W8 5TZ
A Penguin Company
5 7 9 10 8 6 4

Printed in Italy

Parrot
Puzzle

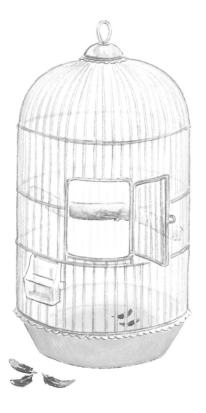

written by Elizabeth Dale
illustrated by David Kearney

"Come on, Tom!" cried Jenny to her friend, running ahead through the woods. It was a beautiful spring day, the sun was shining, the birds were singing, there were trees to be climbed…

"Wait!" called Tom, suddenly.

Jenny stopped and turned. Tom was peering at a bush.

"What is it?" asked Jenny.

"Shh!" whispered Tom. He pointed at the bush. "There's something moving in there."

"Is it a rabbit?" asked Jenny.

Tom frowned. "It's red and yellow and green."

"Go on!" laughed Jenny, who was used to Tom's jokes. "We don't have red and yellow rabbits! Or even green ones."

"But look!" said Tom, pointing.

And then Jenny saw it, too. Something red and yellow was moving in the bushes! She could hardly believe her eyes.

Jenny knelt down and saw a huddle of brightly coloured feathers.

"Oh! It's a parrot!" she whispered.

"What's it doing in the bush?" asked Tom.

"I don't think it can fly," said Jenny.

"Poor thing. Here, boy!" said Tom, stretching out his hand. But the parrot backed away.

7

"We need Dad!" said Jenny.

Her dad was a local vet and any injured animal was taken straight to him. "But we can't leave the parrot alone. Anything might get him."

"I'll get your dad," said Tom. "You stay here and look after the parrot."

"Hurry then!" urged Jenny.

Tom ran off. Jenny stood guard at the bush, talking soothingly to the parrot. But it seemed frightened and fluttered awkwardly into another bush. Why was Tom taking so long? Where was her dad?

Suddenly she heard footsteps. She stood up quickly, ready to protect the injured bird.

"Here we are!" cried Tom.

"Oh, thank goodness!" said Jenny with relief. "Look!"

Mr Walsh was carrying a wicker cage and a towel. He opened up the cage and slowly bent down to look at the parrot.

"You two stay here," he said, taking the towel and walking carefully round the bush. Then he crouched down. Slowly, very slowly, he edged forwards looking anywhere but at the parrot. The bird fluttered about and then looked back at Jenny and Tom. Seizing his chance, Mr Walsh threw the towel over the parrot. Then he quickly put it in the cage.

Back at Greenbanks Surgery
Mr Walsh examined the parrot,
whom Jenny named Humphrey.
There was blood on his feathers and
one wing wouldn't open properly.

"He looks as though he's been in
a fight," said Mr Walsh, bathing
a wound. "And he's very weak.
He's probably escaped from his
owner and can't look after
himself in the wild."

Mr Walsh bent some card to
make a splint for Humphrey's
wing. "There we are," he said.
"It should be mended within
a week. Now we need to get
some food in you."

"Is he going to be all right?" asked Tom, anxiously.

"Yes!" smiled Mr Walsh, removing the elastic band that had held Humphrey's beak closed. "Ouch!" he cried as the bird nipped him. "See, he's getting his strength back already!"

Jenny fetched some bird seed and apples, and Humphrey squawked gleefully when he saw them.

"What's all the noise?" demanded Matthew and Caroline, Jenny's brother and sister.

"Ah! We've got a new pet!" cried Caroline with delight when she saw Humphrey.

"No, we haven't!" said Mr Walsh sternly. "Don't start getting too fond of him. This parrot belongs to someone and we must find out who that someone is."

Jenny smiled. She knew that. Her house had become home to all kinds of sick animals over the years, but only until they were well again. Then they had to go back to where they came from, otherwise their own home would be overrun with animals.

The next day, Mr Walsh let Jenny look after Humphrey. Jenny took his cage into the kitchen and put it down next to a vase of flowers.

"You're really pretty, aren't you?" said Jenny.

"Pretty boy!" cried Humphrey in agreement. "Pretty boy!"

Jenny laughed. "You can talk!"

"Blooming flowers!" squawked Humphrey. "Blooming flowers!"

"What a noise!" cried Jenny's mum, walking in.

"He doesn't like your flowers," giggled Jenny.

"In that case, the sooner we find your owner, Humphrey, the better!" said Mrs Walsh. "I've put a card in the post office window. We'll just have to ask around to see if anyone has lost a parrot."

"Cor, blimey!" said Humphrey, and they laughed.

PARROT FOUND
Please Contact Mr Walsh
at the
Greenbanks Surgery

Jenny loved having Humphrey around. He chatted to her all the time, using some words Jenny had never heard before. But when Jenny tried using them herself she got into trouble!

"That bird has learnt some very bad language!" said Mrs Walsh. "The sooner he goes, the better."

"The better!" agreed Humphrey.

But as the days went by, there was no answer to the card in the post office, and no one knew anyone who had lost a parrot.

"Humphrey is better now," announced Mr Walsh the following Saturday. "He really should be going home. We need his cage for other sick animals."

Jenny was worried. What would happen if they couldn't find Humphrey's owner? Where would he go? If only he could tell them where he had come from.

"Where do you live, Humphrey?"
she asked him.

"Hello, goodbye, blooming flowers!"
said Humphrey.

"Never mind the flowers! They were
here before you!" said Jenny.
"Do you live in a village?
What's it called?"

"Cor, blimey!" said Humphrey.

"Well, that's a lot of help,"
said Jenny.

"Maybe someone at school will
know him," suggested Jenny's mum.
"Why don't you take Humphrey
in to show everyone on Monday?"

"Yes!" cried Jenny.

It was a brilliant idea, and not just because she might discover Humphrey's owner. She couldn't wait to show him off to all her friends.

"Now, no naughty words, Humphrey, or we'll be in serious trouble!" Jenny warned him, as they set off on Monday.

"Naughty words!" agreed Humphrey. "Trouble! Trouble!"

"Exactly!" said Jenny. "So please behave! Mrs King likes everyone to be polite – and that includes parrots!"

But Jenny's teacher loved Humphrey. So did the whole class. They all enjoyed saying 'hello' to him, and the parrot loved saying 'goodbye' back!

"What do you think of school, Humphrey?" asked Mrs King, bending towards his cage.

"Cor, blimey! What a pong!" said Humphrey.

Everyone laughed except Mrs King. She stepped back, looking startled.

"Blooming flowers!" squawked Humphrey gleefully and everyone laughed again.

But then Jenny noticed that there weren't any flowers in the room. Suddenly she had an amazing idea.

As soon as she got home, Jenny ran to the phone book.

"Yippee!" she cried.

"What?" asked her mother.

"Look!" cried Jenny, pointing to the name of a flower shop. "'Blooming Flowers!' That's what Humphrey always says. It might be where he lives!"

"Clever girl!" said Jenny's mum.
She rang the number and a lady
answered.

"Have you by any chance lost a
parrot?" asked Jenny's mum.

"Lorenzo!" cried Miss Simkins, who
owned the flower shop. "Oh! You've
found him! Is he safe?"

Miss Simkins came straight round to collect her parrot. She was so thrilled to see Lorenzo that she cried. Lorenzo flapped around his cage, squawking with glee and calling 'blooming flowers!' at the top of his voice until everyone's head ached.

Jenny was happy for Miss Simkins, but sorry to see Lorenzo go. He'd been great fun to have around. The house would be so quiet without him.

"Goodbye, Humph... I mean Lorenzo," she said sadly, as the parrot hopped into his own cage.

"You must come and visit him," said Miss Simkins. "He'd love to see you, wouldn't you, Lorenzo?"

"Cor, blimey! Blooming flowers!" squawked Lorenzo.

Jenny laughed. How could she be
sad when she still had a friend
like Lorenzo?

Mr Walsh tells you more about... helping injured birds

Almost all birds that do not fly away when you approach them are ill or injured, and they will need to be rescued. If you find a baby bird, it is likely that its mother is nearby and you should leave it alone. Never chase a bird. Instead, move towards it slowly and catch it by throwing a net or some thick material over it.

All birds are checked thoroughly
to find every injury. To make sure
that a broken bone mends
correctly, a vet puts on a
cardboard splint. The cardboard
is folded over the wing and
bandaged in place. After a week,
the vet checks to see if the bone
is mending correctly.

Meet the characters...

Mr Walsh
a vet

Mrs Walsh
a veterinary nurse

Jenny Walsh
nine years old

Matthew Walsh
eleven years old

Caroline Walsh
four years old

Tom Henderson
nine years old and Jenny's best friend

Jepp
the family collie dog

Most injured birds must be given a drink, unless they are going to have an operation straightaway. As with Humphrey, this is best done by a vet putting a tube into the bird's mouth and down into its stomach. Then a special fluid is carefully syringed into the tube. Without this treatment the bird could die.